W9-ANJ-341

EXAMINING ISSUES THROUGH
POLITICAL CARTOONS

Civil Rights

Titles in the Examining Issues Through Political Cartoons series include:

EXAMINING ISSUES THROUGH
POLITICAL CARTOONS

Civil Rights

Edited by Mary E. Williams

Daniel Leone, *President*
Bonnie Szumski, *Publisher*
Scott Barbour, *Managing Editor*

GREENHAVEN PRESS
SAN DIEGO, CALIFORNIA

THOMSON

GALE

Detroit • New York • San Diego • San Francisco
Boston • New Haven, Conn. • Waterville, Maine
London • Munich

No part of this book may be reproduced or used in any form or by any means, electrical, mechanical, or otherwise, including, but not limited to, photocopy, recording, or any information storage and retrieval system, without prior written permission from the publisher.

Library of Congress Cataloging-in-Publication Data

Civil rights / Mary E. Williams, book editor.
    p. cm. — (Examining issues through political cartoons)
Includes bibliographical references and index.
    ISBN 0-7377-1100-0 (lib. : alk. paper)
    ISBN 0-7377-1099-3 (pbk. : alk. paper)
    1. African Americans—Civil rights—History—Caricatures and cartoons. 2. Minorities—Civil rights—United States—History—Caricatures and cartoons. 3. Civil rights movements—United States—History—Caricatures and cartoons. 4. United States—Race relations—Caricatures and cartoons. 5. American wit and humor, Pictorial. I. Williams, Mary E., 1960–   II. Series.

E185.61 .C5915 2002
323.1'196073'00207—dc21

                                                  2001055742

Cover photo: Wright. © 1995 Tribune Media Services.
Reprinted with permission.

Copyright © 2002 by Greenhaven Press,
an imprint of The Gale Group
10911 Technology Place
San Diego, CA 92127
Printed in the U.S.A.

Contents

Foreword

Political cartoons, also called editorial cartoons, are drawings that do what editorials do with words—express an opinion about a newsworthy event or person. They typically appear in the opinion pages of newspapers, sometimes in support of that day's written editorial, but more often making their own comment on the day's events. Political cartoons first gained widespread popularity in Great Britain and the United States in the 1800s when engravings and other drawings skewering political figures were fashionable in illustrated newspapers and comic magazines. By the beginning of the 1900s, editorial cartoons were an established feature of daily newspapers. Today, they can be found throughout the globe in newspapers, magazines, and online publications on the Internet.

Art Wood, both a cartoonist and a collector of cartoons, writes in his book *Great Cartoonists and Their Art*:

> Day in and day out the cartoonist mirrors history; he reduces complex facts into understandable and artistic terminology. He is a political commentator and at the same time an artist.

The distillation of ideas into images is what makes political cartoons a valuable resource for studying social and historical topics. Editorial cartoons have a point to express. Analyzing them involves determining both what the cartoon's point is and how it was made.

Sometimes, the point made by the cartoon may be one that the reader disagrees with, or considers offensive. Such cartoons expose readers to new ideas and thereby challenge them to analyze and question their own opinions and assumptions. In some extreme cases, cartoons provide vivid examples of the thoughts that lie behind heinous acts; for example, the cartoons created by the Nazis illustrate the anti-Semitism that led to the mass persecution of Jews.

Examining controversial ideas is but one way the study of political cartoons can enhance and develop critical thinking skills. Another aspect to cartoons is that they can use symbols to make their point quickly. For example, in a cartoon in *Euthanasia*, Chuck Asay depicts supporters of a legal "right to die" by assisted suicide as vultures. Vultures are birds that eat dead and dying animals and are often a symbol of repulsive and cowardly predators who take advantage of those who have met misfortune or are vulnerable. The reader can infer that Asay is expressing his opposition to physician-assisted suicide by suggesting that its supporters are just as loathsome as vultures. Asay thus makes his point through a quick symbolic association.

An important part of critical thinking is examining ideas and arguments in their historical context. Political cartoonists (reasonably) assume that the typical reader of a newspaper's editorial page already has a basic knowledge of current issues and newsworthy people. Understanding and appreciating political cartoons often requires such knowledge, as well as a familiarity with common icons and symbolic figures (such as Uncle Sam's representing the United States). The need for contextual information becomes especially apparent in historical cartoons. For example, although most people know who Adolf Hitler is, a lack of familiarity with other German political figures of the 1930s may create difficulty in fully understanding cartoons about Nazi Germany made in that era.

Providing such contextual information is one important way that Greenhaven's Examining Issues Through Political Cartoons series seeks to make this unique and revealing resource conveniently accessible to students. Each volume presents a representative and diverse collection of political cartoons focusing on a particular current or historical topic. An introductory essay provides a general overview of the subject matter. Each cartoon is then presented with accompanying information including facts about the cartoonist and information and commentary on the cartoon itself. Finally, each volume contains additional informational resources, including listings of books, articles, and websites; an index; and (for historical topics) a chronology of events. Taken together, the contents of each anthology constitute an amusing and informative resource for students of historical and social topics.

Introduction

The phrase "civil rights" often conjures up compelling images of the protests and marches that were the hallmark of the mid–twentieth century movement to end racial segregation and garner social and political rights for African Americans. However, the fight for civil rights began long before the grassroots demonstrations of the 1950s and 1960s, and many of today's social analysts would maintain that the struggle is far from over. While "civil rights" in a general sense refers to the constitutional and legal rights enjoyed by all citizens, most discussions on the subject focus on the history of antiblack discrimination in America. Although the plights of women, ethnic and religious minorities, disabled people, and gays and lesbians have also motivated battles for equal rights, the status of African Americans has been the source of much of the controversy and legislation involving civil rights in the United States.

The struggle for civil rights in America began with the earliest resistance by blacks to their forced arrival in the colonies and their ensuing subjugation and unequal treatment. Some slaves silently protested their involuntary servitude by slowing the pace of their labor, sabotaging their work, or running away. In the 1770s, the colonial push for independence that culminated in the Revolutionary War coincided with an increased eagerness for liberty and self-determination among slaves as well as free blacks. Free blacks living in the North and upper South, for example, formed organizations that confronted racial discrimination through petitions, boycotts, and economic self-protection. One such organization was Boston's African Society, first established in 1796, whose members collected dues—in essence, a kind of life insurance—to protect their heirs lest changing circumstances force them into slavery. In 1797 a group of

North Carolina blacks who had been freed by their masters petitioned the U.S. House of Representatives to protect them from roving bands of whites intent on collecting the rewards offered for capturing fugitive slaves. Their petition was unsuccessful, but it inspired certain segments of the antislavery movement in the 1800s.

Nineteenth-Century Developments

In the nineteenth century, free blacks in the North found themselves increasingly restricted in the job market. Because craft and trade unions would not accept African Americans, they were usually limited to unskilled labor or jobs as domestics—work that became more difficult to procure as the white immigrant laborer population grew. In addition, free blacks in the North and the South were not allowed to attend most public schools, a situation which further hindered their economic mobility. Northern blacks, however, were able to express their grievances with a degree of freedom that was denied to southern blacks. This is evident in the emergence of several newspapers edited by northern blacks, such as *Freedom's Journal*, first published in New York City in 1827, which gave voice to the sufferings and the hopes of African Americans. Another instrument of protest in the North was the black church. Many African American clergymen interpreted the message of the Christian Gospel as a divine call for liberty, justice, and equality. Moreover, the black church was instrumental in spawning the African American convention movement, another avenue of organized protest in the North. At the first convention in 1830, participants spoke out strongly against the popular idea—backed by Americans of various political persuasions—that free blacks should be moved to Africa or Central America to eliminate racial problems in the United States.

The leading organization that advocated repatriating free blacks was the American Colonization Society (ACS), founded in the early 1800s. The ACS was unusual in that it drew the support of some southern slaveholders as well as black and white northerners. Some southerners believed that deporting freed slaves would make it easier to maintain legalized slavery. Many northerners, on the other hand, felt that the relocation of ex-slaves might make slaveholders less reluctant to free them; they also surmised that northern and southern whites might become less fearful about the potential consequences of emancipation. "Appealing simultaneously to those who hated or feared free blacks and those who deplored or regretted American racism," notes historian Lewis Perry, "removal schemes raised hopes of forging an irresistible coalition that might, once and for all, end slavery."

Although the ACS did send a few thousand blacks to its acquired colony, Liberia, it failed to obtain federal funding for its cause, and support for recolonization efforts slowly dwindled after 1830. A majority of black leaders rejected repatriation, protesting the ACS's portrayal of African Americans as a "dangerous and useless" class. Militant black abolitionists such as David Walker argued that "the colonizing plan" was rooted in the same racism that had resulted in black enslavement and "wretchedness." In his provocative 1829 document *Appeal*, Walker also called for slaves to rebel against their masters, contending that "slavery is ten thousand times more injurious to this country than all the other evils put together. . . . I tell you Americans! that unless you speedily alter your course, *you* and your *Country are gone!!!!!* For God Almighty will tear up the very face of the earth!!!"

It became clear, however, that blacks could not topple the institution of slavery or ideas such as those held by the ACS on their own. After the publication of Walker's *Appeal*, southern states quickly passed laws forbidding anyone to teach slaves to read or write—an attempt to keep revolutionary ideas away from a slave audience. News about violent slave rebellions, particularly Nat Turner's 1831 insurrection, intensified slaveholders' fear of free blacks and abolitionist sentiments. By the mid-1830s, slaveholders were demanding the extradition of abolitionist leaders to the South for trial and offered to pay bounties for them dead or alive. Black leaders came to see that they would need to build coalitions with strong white allies to fight slavery and racial discrimination.

One such ally was William Lloyd Garrison. In the early 1830s, Garrison dropped his membership in the ACS and founded the American Anti-Slavery Society, which adopted the position that slavery had to be immediately abolished "through moral and political action." Abolitionist societies were nothing new; many were formed in the 1780s. But after northern states abolished slavery—and after Congress banned the foreign slave trade in 1808—many white abolitionists had assumed that the institution of slavery in the United States would collapse of its own accord. Consequently, abolition societies lost membership and direction until the 1830s, when "immediatist" abolitionists such as Garrison took up the antislavery cause with revivalist fervor. Garrison's Boston-based newspaper, the *Liberator*, drew a large readership of northern blacks who appreciated Garrison's assertion that "no man has a right to enslave or imbrute his brother . . . or to brutalize his mind by denying him the means of intellectual, social, and moral improvement. The right to enjoy liberty is inalienable. To invade it is to usurp the prerogative of Jehovah."

The American Anti-Slavery Society spawned several other interracial abolitionist organizations. Some of the most notable contributions to the revitalized antislavery movement came from fugitive slaves such as Frederick Douglass and Harriet Tubman, who spoke at meetings and shared firsthand accounts of the experience of slavery even when they were in danger of being recognized, caught, and sent back into bondage. Tubman herself helped dozens of slaves to escape by organizing the Underground Railroad and helping fugitives establish new lives in the North.

Several black abolitionists wrote influential articles, narratives, and speeches about the horrors of slavery as well as the discrimination faced by free blacks in the North. One black Anti-Slavery Society member, Charles Lenox Remond, addressed a legislative committee in the Massachusetts House of Representatives in 1842 to protest racial segregation on the railroads. During his speech, he contrasted the humane and nondiscriminatory treatment he received during his travels in Europe with the segregation he faced upon his return home. In his closing remarks, he argued that blacks had already earned the right to be treated as full citizens:

> If colored people have abused any rights granted them, or failed to exhibit due appreciation of favors bestowed, or shrunk from dangers or responsibility, let it be made to appear. Or if our country contains a population to compare with them in loyalty and patriotism, circumstances duly considered, I have it yet to learn. The history of our country must ever testify in their behalf. In view of these and many additional considerations, I unhesitatingly assert their claim, on the naked principle of merit, to every advantage set forth in the Constitution of this Commonwealth.

One year later, as a result of Remond's petition, the Massachusetts legislature abolished railway segregation. Another antidiscrimination effort in Massachusetts also met with success: Blacks and sympathetic whites staged a series of boycotts from 1844 to 1855 that pressured Boston leaders to desegregate public schools.

Despite these victories, blacks in the first half of the nineteenth century found that their struggle for even a limited array of civil rights was increasingly restricted by legislation. By the 1840s, all but five northern states had curbed or abolished the right of free blacks to vote. In 1850, Congress passed the Fugitive Slave Law, which allowed any black person living in the North to be sent South on the strength of a claim by anyone testifying to be his or her owner. The law also denied runaway slaves the right to defend themselves in court and to trials by jury, and it exacted heavy fines from anyone harboring runaway slaves or interfering with the capture of escaped slaves. In practice, this law meant that free blacks could easily be sold into slavery. Many northerners—even those who had previously believed that the issue of slavery should be decided at the state level—were alarmed by the Fugitive Slave Law, fearing that it gave the South too much power over individual rights.

The state of civil rights protections for blacks and other people of color reached its lowest point with the 1857 case of *Dred Scott v. Sanford*. Dred Scott was a slave who had filed an 1847 lawsuit claiming that he deserved to be considered a free man because he had traveled and lived in Illinois, a free state, and free portions of the Louisiana Territory. The Supreme Court ruled that the U.S. Constitution granted citizenship to whites only, and that nonwhites had no rights under federal law. The Court also denied Congress the power to ban slavery in any federal territory. Northern abolitionists were appalled by the *Dred Scott* decision, and the nation became more sharply divided over the question of slavery.

In 1856 one of the political offshoots of the American Anti-Slavery Society, the Free Soil Party, adopted the abolition slogan "Free soil, free speech, free labor, and free men." The Free Soil Party was one of the precursors of the Republican Party, which came to national prominence in 1860 when Abraham Lincoln was elected president. During his campaign, Lincoln had called for a ban on expanding slavery into new U.S. territories, but had stopped short of proposing an immediate end to the institution in the South. Southerners, however, considered Lincoln to be a staunch abolitionist. Starting in December 1860, thirteen Southern states seceded from the Union and formed the Confederacy—partly in response to Lincoln's election as president. After the Civil War began in 1861, Lincoln repeatedly stressed that the purpose of the conflict was to preserve the Union, not to liberate the slaves. The Emancipation Proclamation that he issued in 1862—a document freeing all slaves living in Confederate states as of January 1, 1863—was more an attempt to turn the tide of the war in favor of the North than a push for abolitionist reforms. Nevertheless, with many white Northerners acclaiming the proclamation, and with blacks viewing it as a harbinger of freedom, the war became a crusade to eradicate slavery. With the Union victory in April 1865 and the ratification of the Thirteenth Amendment in December 1865, slavery was outlawed in all states, effecting a triumph for the abolitionists.

The Reconstruction Era

Immediately after the Civil War, southern legislatures began enacting the "black codes," harshly discriminatory laws that were modeled after the slave codes that had existed before the war. These codes specified what sort of work African Americans could and could not do and established penalties, including hard labor, for black unemployment, vagrancy, and curfew violations. Intended to maintain the racial caste system that southern whites had long been accustomed to, the codes defined ex-slaves as second-class citizens and essentially returned them to a state of bondage.

Recognizing that the black codes were an attempt to nullify emancipation, the Republican majority in Congress took steps to secure the freedom of ex-slaves through legislation at the federal level. The result was an unprecedented blossoming of civil rights protections for African Americans. The Civil Rights Act of 1866 granted full citizenship to all people born in the United States (except for Native Americans, who were not subject to taxes). This act laid the groundwork for the Fourteenth Amendment, which proclaimed that "all persons born . . . in the United States are citizens of the United States and the State wherein they reside" and that states could not deny any individual's right to life, liberty, or property without due process of law. In 1867, Congress began passing a series of Reconstruction Acts, one of which gave southern black men the right to vote and hold political office; another required the former Confederate states to ratify the Fourteenth Amendment before rejoining the Union.

Several other civil rights measures quickly followed. In 1870, Congress approved the Fifteenth Amendment, which stated that American citizens could not be denied the right to vote because of their race, color, or former status as a slave. When the Ku Klux Klan and other southern terrorist groups mounted violent campaigns to deter former slaves from voting or exercising other rights guaranteed to them as citizens, Congress passed a series of Enforcement Acts (also known as the Ku Klux Acts) in 1870 and 1871. These measures authorized federal supervision of elections, allowed the use of the U.S. Army to curb Klan activity, and exacted stiff penalties from any individual who used intimidation and violence to keep people from voting or from exercising any other constitutionally protected right. The Enforcement Acts brought a modicum of peace and order to the recovering South, and several black men were elected to the U.S. Senate and House of Representatives.

In 1875, Congress passed an ambitious Civil Rights Act that outlawed racial discrimination in public transportation and in public places such as restaurants, hotels, and theaters, as well as on juries. The majority of blacks, however, were too poor to take advantage of these rights. The southern-dominated Supreme Court, moreover, had already begun to restrict the federal government's power to protect civil rights. The Court had ruled in a series of 1873 cases that state citizenship, not U.S. citizenship, was the source of most individual rights, in effect limiting federal protection of individual rights. In the 1876 case of *United States v. Cruikshank*, the Supreme Court declared that the Fourteenth Amendment did not protect blacks from personal infringements on their rights, only from state infringements. This ruling had the effect of nullifying the Enforcement Acts, making it difficult for the federal government to protect African Americans from private acts of discrimination and violence. This ruling also paved the way for post-Reconstruction southern legislatures to pass state laws that would legalize racial discrimination and segregation.

The Beginning of the Jim Crow Era
With the end of Reconstruction in 1877, conservative white Democrats regained control of southern state governments and began

to enact measures intended to maintain white dominance in the region. In 1881, Tennessee became the first state to adopt a "Jim Crow" law requiring the separation of whites and blacks in railway coaches. Other southern states soon followed suit, drafting legislation requiring racial segregation in schools, hospitals, transportation, and public accommodations. In 1883 the U.S. Supreme Court overturned the Civil Rights Act of 1875—the measure that had previously outlawed racial discrimination in public places. The Court claimed that the act was unconstitutional because "equal protection of the law" could not apply to social privileges such as nondiscriminatory treatment in public places.

Black voting rights also came under attack during the post-Reconstruction era. Several southern states began adopting laws requiring potential voters to pay poll taxes or pass certain literacy and "comprehension" tests before registering. Discriminatory enforcement of these measures by bigoted white officials led to the disfranchisement of blacks at the voting booth. In 1890 a group of black delegates from forty Mississippi counties met with President Benjamin Harrison to protest the pending loss of their right to vote, but the president refused to intervene. By the end of the nineteenth century, after the Supreme Court had upheld the right of states to require literacy tests and poll taxes as a prerequisite for voting, only 2 percent of black males in Mississippi and Alabama were registered to vote.

Many African Americans used the legal system to confront the South's new discriminatory laws. Black train passenger Homer Plessy, for example, challenged Louisiana's statute requiring separate railroad cars for whites and blacks after he was arrested for refusing to leave a whites-only car. When a state judge ruled against him, Plessy appealed to the U.S. Supreme Court, which resulted in the famous 1896 *Plessy v. Ferguson* case. In *Plessy*, the Court ruled that state governments could require separate public accommodations for whites and blacks, as long as the accommodations were "equal." Although the majority of justices agreed that the Fourteenth Amendment did guarantee certain rights to blacks, they maintained that it "could not have been intended to abolish distinctions based on color, or to enforce social . . . equality or [to bring about a mixing] of the two races upon terms unsatisfactory to either."

The *Plessy* ruling established a legal foundation for Jim Crow segregation that was to last until the middle of the twentieth century.

Supreme Court justice John Harlan, who opposed the *Plessy* decision, predicted that legalized segregation would encourage misguided notions about race and lead to more daily discrimination against African Americans and an increasing erosion of black rights. This was already proving to be true in the 1880s and 1890s, as the lynching of blacks in the South reached epidemic proportions, with few attempts to protect potential victims or bring perpetrators to justice. In 1892 alone, 241 lynchings were reported. By 1907 every southern state had laws requiring the separation of blacks and whites in almost all areas of life, leading to a deeper entrenchment of racial intolerance among many southerners.

Life for black northerners was somewhat less harsh than it was for southern blacks. In the North, African Americans were generally not barred from voting, and laws requiring segregation were rare. Still, northern statutes that banned racial discrimination in public places were not strongly enforced, and white-owned hotels, theaters, and restaurants often refused to serve blacks.

From Accommodation to Activism

In the South of the late nineteenth and early twentieth centuries—a period when lynchings and other forms of intimidation against blacks were commonplace—direct forms of protest against racial discrimination were generally too dangerous to attempt. Instead, many African Americans adopted a gradualist, accommodationist approach to race relations, one that emphasized hard work and vocational training among blacks as a way to slowly win the respect of whites. At the turn of the twentieth century, Booker T. Washington was the leading proponent of this approach. Born a slave, Washington was the principal of Alabama's Tuskegee Institute, one of the first vocational schools for blacks in the South. He was also one of the most sought-after speakers on the topic of race relations and the importance of job training for blacks.

In 1895, Washington was invited to participate in the Cotton States International Exposition in Atlanta, Georgia, where he delivered one of the first major addresses by a black man to a mostly white southern audience, his controversial "Atlanta Compromise" speech. Washington encouraged southern whites to support the vocational training of blacks; in turn, he urged blacks to be patient and abandon demands for equal rights, maintaining that these rights would be earned over time:

> The wisest among my race understand that the agitation of questions of social equality is the extremest of folly, and that progress in the enjoyment of all the privileges that will come to us must be the result of severe and constant struggle rather than of artificial forcing. . . . It is important and right that all privileges of the law be ours, but it is vastly more important that we be prepared for the exercise of these privileges.

Right after his 1895 speech, Washington was hailed by the white public as "a prominent and sensible man" and a "progressive Negro educator"; many blacks also saw him as an articulate and responsible spokesperson. But within a few years, some African American thinkers took note of the deteriorating status of blacks in the South and began to challenge the philosophy of accommodation. One such critic, Harvard-educated W.E.B. Du Bois, questioned the assumption that blacks could advance before being granted civil rights: "Is it possible . . . that nine millions of men can make effective progress in economic lines if they are deprived of political rights, made a servile caste, and allowed only the most meagre chance for developing their exceptional men? If history and reason give any distinct answer to these questions, it is an emphatic *No.*" Du Bois came to believe that Washington's gradualism was helping to perpetuate the Jim Crow oppression of blacks in the South. He was also disheartened by Washington's emphasis on vocational training, believing that college-level education would better prepare blacks for equality with whites.

In 1905, Du Bois and several other African American intellectuals met near Niagara Falls, Canada, to organize opposition to Washington's accommodationist tactics. Establishing a short-lived group known as the Niagara Movement, the organizers resolved to protest racial discrimination, work to reinstitute black voting rights, and demand full equality for all black Americans: "We shall not be satisfied with less than full manhood rights. . . .We claim for ourselves every right that belongs to a free-born American—political, civil, and social—and until we get these rights, we shall never cease to protest and assail the ears of America with the story of its shameful deeds toward us." Booker T. Washington vehemently opposed the Niagara group and used his political influence to hinder its development. Within three years, the group dissolved.

Washington had not seen the end of challenges to his philosophy, however. In August 1908, a violent race riot occurred in Springfield, Illinois. The shock of having such a disturbance take place in the birthplace of Abraham Lincoln caused concerned white philanthropists to call a conference for all those who wished to assist African Americans in the cause of racial equality. In 1909 a group of white social workers, labor activists, and descendants of abolitionists invited several black intellectuals—most of whom had been involved in the Niagara Movement—to join them in forming a new civil rights organization: the National Association for the Advancement of Colored People (NAACP). The group adopted the Niagara Movement's activist platform of demanding equal educational, political, and civil rights for blacks and the enforcement of the Fourteenth and Fifteenth Amendments.

The NAACP pursued a strategy of publicity, lobbying, and litigation to achieve its goals. Its earliest efforts included an aggressive antilynching campaign involving congressional bills, published studies, leaflets, educational forums, and silent protest marches to garner federal and public support for ending mob violence against blacks. Although Congress never passed an antilynching law, the NAACP campaign raised public awareness about lynching and led to a decrease in the crime. By the second decade of the twentieth century, NAACP lawyers were successfully arguing Supreme Court cases. In the 1915 case of *Guinn v. U.S.*, for example, the Court outlawed the "grandfather clause," a device southern states had employed to exempt white voters from the literacy tests that were used to keep blacks from voting. Two years later, in *Buchanan v. Warley*, the Court struck down laws requiring the racial segregation of residential neighborhoods. Although the rulings in these cases had little immediate effect on black voting rights or residential segregation, they set the tone for a series of NAACP legal successes that would to profoundly affect American race relations later in the twentieth century.

The NAACP's first dramatic accomplishment was its 1930 battle to defeat President Herbert Hoover's nomination of Judge John J. Parker to the Supreme Court. In a previous political campaign,

Parker had spoken against black voting rights. By forming coalitions with other influential groups, the NAACP managed to lobby just enough senators to block Parker's confirmation. Through the rest of the 1930s, NAACP lawyers Charles Hamilton Houston and Thurgood Marshall developed a legal strategy intended to provoke fundamental change. Noting that the Supreme Court was becoming increasingly sympathetic to civil rights, Houston and Marshall focused on using the "separate but equal" doctrine of *Plessy* to challenge the racial inequities in the South's segregated school system. Their campaign initially targeted higher education, where discrimination was most evident. Specifically, southern states would not allow African Americans to attend their graduate and professional schools, but there were no comparable programs in the region's black colleges. By evoking Court rulings that would force states to create "equal" curricula in white *and* black schools, the NAACP hoped to make segregated education too expensive and cumbersome for the South to maintain.

The strategy worked, ultimately calling into question the notion that segregated education could be truly equal. From 1935 to 1950, a series of Supreme Court rulings required several states to create graduate and professional schools for blacks. When the states did so, the Court then ordered that these schools be wholly equal to those that whites attended. In the 1950 case of *Sweatt v. Painter*, a black applicant was allowed admittance to the University of Texas Law School when the Court found that state's black law school was inferior. This ruling brought the NAACP and the Supreme Court closer to dismantling Jim Crow education entirely.

The NAACP's legal teams won several other victories against discrimination in the 1940s and 1950s. In the 1944 case of *Smith v. Allwright*, all-white election primaries were declared unconstitutional, and in the 1946 case of *Morgan v. Virginia*, the Supreme Court outlawed racial segregation on interstate buses and trains. Again, these rulings had little effect on the day-to-day life of African Americans because they were rarely enforced. The mood of the country began to shift, however, as northern Democrats expressed increasing support for civil rights. The Democratic Party had experienced an upsurge of liberal political participation in the 1930s, a development that attracted many African Americans to the party. After World War II, when northern Democrats faced stiff challenges from Republican candidates, they took a more aggressive stance on civil rights to help keep blacks in the party. In 1948, Democratic president Harry S. Truman issued an executive order calling for equal opportunity for all Americans in the U.S. armed forces, effectively banning racial segregation in the military. For many civil rights advocates, the country seemed on the verge of great change.

The Civil Rights Movement

In the landmark 1954 case of *Brown v. Board of Education*, the Supreme Court declared school segregation unconstitutional, arguing that racially separate education was inherently unequal. The Court stopped short of completely overturning the 1896 *Plessy* ruling on "separate but equal" public facilities; nevertheless, the *Brown* ruling was the spark that ignited the modern civil rights movement—an upsurge of grassroots political activity aimed at overturning segregation laws in the South and obtaining social and political rights for African Americans in all states. From the mid-1950s through the end of the 1960s, civil rights activists staged boycotts, protests, and demonstrations to support desegregation, and their efforts resulted in a host of new federal laws that outlawed racial discrimination in housing, employment, and public accommodations. Before these new laws were drafted and enacted, however, the grassroots activists faced massive opposition in both the North and the South.

The Supreme Court recognized that the *Brown* ruling would face intense resistance in the South and in 1956 tried to temper opposition by ordering desegregation to proceed "with all deliberate speed"—in other words, gradually and cautiously. Southern senators and representatives responded by declaring that they would use "all lawful means" to reverse the school desegregation order. Local school districts, as well as a significant segment of the public, vehemently opposed school integration. Crowds often turned out to jeer and heckle black students on the first day of a desegregated school year. On several occasions, federal troops had to be called in to accompany black students to school. A few districts closed all their public schools rather than give in to the desegregation order.

Seeing that large numbers of whites—including many public officials and state representatives—would continue to concoct ways to evade court-ordered desegregation, many civil rights supporters decided that direct confrontation was needed to stir the conscience of America. In 1955, Rosa Parks, a former secretary for the Montgomery, Alabama, NAACP, was arrested for refusing to give up her seat to a white passenger on a segregated city bus. The incident triggered a year-long boycott of the Montgomery bus system, led by recently ordained Baptist minister Martin Luther King Jr. Federal courts eventually ordered Montgomery to integrate its buses, and the national attention the boycott received alerted many to the continuing discrimination faced by black Americans. Moreover, the boycott's success encouraged other activists to apply King's nonviolent tactics in other places where local laws supported racial segregation.

King was first attracted to the notion of nonviolent direct action in college when he was introduced to the ideas of Henry David Thoreau and Mohandas Gandhi. Thoreau's essay "Civil Disobedience" convinced King of the virtue of refusing to cooperate with unjust laws, while Gandhi's strategy of direct but peaceful confrontation with authorities influenced King's ideas on nonviolent social change. King aimed to fuse Thoreau's and Gandhi's ideas with the Christian principles of loving one's enemies and turning the other cheek. He described his nonviolent philosophy during a speech at the beginning of the 1955 Montgomery bus boycott:

> We cannot in all good conscience obey your unjust laws and abide by the unjust system, because noncooperation with evil is as much a moral obligation as is cooperation with good, and so throw us in jail and we will still love you. Bomb our homes and threaten our children . . . and we will still love you. But be assured that we'll wear you down by our capacity to suffer, and one day we will win our freedom. We will not only win freedom for ourselves, we will so appeal to your heart and conscience that we will win you in the process, and our victory will be a double victory.

The activists galvanized by King were not the first to advocate peaceful direct action. In Chicago in 1942, the Congress of Racial Equality (CORE) had been founded as a northern interracial organization that would oppose racial discrimination through demonstrations, picketing, and nonviolent confrontation combined with goodwill toward the adversary. In 1943, CORE had staged the first civil rights "sit-in" at a "whites-only" Chicago restaurant, during which interracial groups of activists ordered food and refused to leave until the African Americans among them were served. In 1947, CORE had sent the first integrated bus of "freedom riders" to the upper South to test whether court-ordered desegregation in interstate travel had taken effect. The supporters that gathered around King, however, were to form the first South-wide civil rights organization: the Southern Christian Leadership Conference (SCLC), established in 1957. The SCLC pledged to pursue a combined strategy of nonviolent direct action, litigation, boycotts, and black voter registration.

The presence of a southern-rooted civil rights organization emboldened grassroots activists, and the pace of political change accelerated in the 1960s. In February 1960, four African American college students staged a sit-in at a lunch counter in Greensboro, North Carolina. By the following week, CORE began organizing similar sit-ins in fifteen southern cities, spawning what was to be a two-year sit-in movement that desegregated many public facilities in the South. The movement received high-level support in July 1960, when the Democratic National Convention adopted a civil rights platform that endorsed school desegregation, demonstrations, and sit-ins.

In the spring of 1960, a group of college students involved with the sit-in movement founded the Student Nonviolent Coordinating Committee (SNCC, pronounced "snick"). SNCC field volunteers engaged in some of the most challenging and dangerous civil rights activism by moving into communities in the Deep South to help the region's blacks register to vote. They also took over CORE's "freedom rides" in 1961 after CORE members encountered bus bombings, beatings, and arrests in Alabama. Civil rights workers in the early 1960s had to learn to steel themselves against the violence and brutal treatment they would face in the deep South.

This violence drew national attention in April 1963, when Martin Luther King and other civil rights leaders initiated a protest campaign to desegregate public facilities in Birmingham, Alabama. The city's openly racist police chief, Eugene "Bull" Connor, encouraged police to turn fire hoses and police dogs on a large crowd of nonviolent demonstrators, many of them children from local schools. Hundreds of demonstrators were beaten and arrested. The violent commotion, which was broadcast in national and world news media, horrified Americans across the country.

The explicit media coverage had the effect that civil rights leaders had hoped for. Through television, millions of people witnessed the startling brutality of racist oppression for the first time, and support for the movement grew in both the North and the South. In June 1963, President John Kennedy appeared on national television, focusing much of his speech on the civil rights issue and announcing his support for new legislation:

> The fires of frustration and discord are busy in every city. Redress is sought in the street, in demonstrations, parades and protests which create tensions and threaten violence. We face, therefore, a moral crisis as a country and as a people. I am therefore asking the Congress to enact legislation giving all Americans the right to be served in facilities which are open to the public. . . . This seems to me to be an elementary right. Its denial is an arbitrary indignity that no American in 1963 should have to endure.

From June through August 1963, civil rights protests occurred in nearly every major city in the United States. To exhibit growing public support for the civil rights legislation that Kennedy had proposed, the SCLC, CORE, SNCC, and the NAACP convened with church and labor groups to organize a massive late-summer demonstration, a "March on Washington." On August 28, 1963, more than 250,000 demonstrators assembled at the base of the Washington Monument to participate in a march to the Lincoln Memorial, where several civil rights leaders delivered speeches. This event—the largest single protest demonstration in U.S. history—culminated in Martin Luther King's famous "I Have a Dream" speech. "It was a speech of hope and determination, epitomizing the day's message of racial harmony, love, unity, and a belief that blacks and whites could live together in peace," notes journalist Juan Williams. "The event was a resounding success. . . . Many Americans witnessed for the first time black people and white united, marching and celebrating side by side."

Within a year of the March on Washington, Congress passed the Civil Rights Act of 1964—the most sweeping legislation of its kind since the Reconstruction era—forbidding discrimination in jobs, housing, and public accommodations because of race, color, religion, sex, or national origin. The civil rights movement had certainly passed a major milestone with the enactment of this legislation, but the struggle was far from over. As was the case with court-ordered school desegregation, it was apparent that bigoted and racist attitudes would change much more slowly than laws would. Civil rights activists and sympathizers still faced violence and threats of violence, particularly in the Deep South. In June 1963, the day after Kennedy's televised speech, Mississippi's NAACP field director, Medgar Evers, was assassinated. In September 1963, less than a month after the March on Washington, four black girls were killed in the bombing of the Sixteenth Street Baptist Church—a center of civil rights activism—in Birmingham, Alabama. Southern blacks attempting to register to vote, moreover, still encountered fierce resistance from local officials.

In 1964, SNCC declared a "freedom summer," inviting more than one thousand northern students to help register black voters in Mississippi and to teach in their "freedom schools." Many of these activists were arrested, jailed, and brutally beaten. Reports of racial violence began surfacing in the news media with frightening regularity. On August 4, 1964, the bodies of three SNCC volunteers—two white and one black—were discovered near Philadelphia, Mississippi. Local segregationists and law enforcement officers were implicated in the murders. On August 22, 1964, Fannie Lou Hamer, a Mississippi sharecropper and political activist, testified on national television about the treatment of southern blacks who tried to register to vote. She stunned the nation with her description of how a highway patrolman arrested her after a voter-registration workshop, took her to a county jail, and forced two black prisoners to bludgeon her until they were exhausted. During a 1965 SCLC campaign to register black voters in Alabama, a black demonstrator and a white minister died after being beaten by state troopers and counterprotesters.

The need to strengthen governmental authority to counter discriminatory practices by southern election officials was sorely evident. In May 1965, Congress passed the Voting Rights Act of 1965, which banned the use of poll taxes and literacy tests as a prerequisite for voting. The new law also enabled federal officials to register eligible voters if local officials refused to do so. As a result of the

Voting Rights Act, southern black participation in elections increased dramatically.

Divisions Within the Civil Rights Movement

Not everyone involved in the struggle for black civil rights supported the nonviolent direct action tactics espoused by Martin Luther King, the SCLC, and the NAACP. By the mid-1960s, many African Americans, particularly the young and the poor living in northern cities, were frustrated by the economic inequities and discrimination that continued despite the passage of antidiscrimination laws. Many were also angered by the bombings, murders, and other brutal reactions to the voter registration drives and the federal government's failure to protect the rights of activists. Some blacks, disillusioned with the idea of petitioning a white-dominated political system for basic human rights, came to believe that equality could not be attained through peaceful confrontation and racial integration. They turned instead to a philosophy of black self-reliance, self-defense, and militant nationalism as a means to achieve black liberation.

The most celebrated proponent of black nationalism was Malcolm X, an articulate, outspoken organizer who had developed his views under the tutelage of the Nation of Islam. For much of the twentieth century, this black Muslim sect had taught that whites were inherently evil and that African Americans could lift themselves out of degradation through education and faith in Allah. Although Malcolm X eventually broke with the Nation of Islam and reexamined his attitude toward whites, his speeches usually emphasized black pride and a refusal to "turn the other cheek" to oppression. In an interview with psychologist Kenneth Clark, for example, Malcolm X contended that "any Negro who teaches Negroes to turn the other cheek in the face of attack is disarming that Negro of his God-given right, of his moral right, of his natural right, of his intelligent right to defend himself." In his famous 1964 "Ballot or the Bullet" speech, he stated, "Black people are fed up with the dillydallying, pussyfooting, compromising approach that we've been using toward getting our freedom. We want freedom *now*, but we're not going to get it saying 'We Shall Overcome.' We've got to fight until we overcome."

By the time of his assassination in 1965, Malcolm X had begun to mobilize an array of followers who were ready to take a more aggressive stand on procuring rights for African Americans. One of these followers was Stokely Carmichael, a young African American who became the leader of SNCC in 1966. During the June 1966 civil rights "March Against Fear"—a three-week protest march from Memphis, Tennessee, to Jackson, Mississippi—Carmichael used the phrase "black power" in a speech, endorsing the possibility of using any means, even violence, to combat racial discrimination. Martin Luther King, who was also participating in the March Against Fear, disagreed with Carmichael and convinced him to avoid publicly discussing black power for the duration of the protest. But the notion struck a nerve among many civil rights activists. In July 1966, CORE approved the concept of black power at its national convention. In December 1966, SNCC expelled its white activists and announced its transformation into a separatist black nationalist organization.

While CORE and SNCC grew increasingly militant, other black nationalist groups emerged. The most famous of these new groups, the Black Panthers, formed in 1967 with the initial intention of patrolling black neighborhoods to defend African Americans from police brutality. Their radical rhetoric—"total liberty for black people or total destruction for America"—and heavily armed, macho demeanor created a public image that tended to obscure the success of their community-service programs that offered free health care, food, and education to poor blacks. The Black Panthers accepted whites as allies in the black liberation struggle as long as they understood that blacks would be the leaders of the movement. For a few months in 1968, SNCC merged with the Panthers. The two groups separated over a disagreement about the role of whites in the black power movement.

In the late 1960s, FBI director J. Edgar Hoover launched a campaign to "expose, disrupt, misdirect, discredit, or otherwise neutralize the activities of black nationalist, hate-type organizations and groupings." Undercover FBI agents infiltrated black nationalist groups and civil rights organizations to create discord and infighting. Several Black Panthers were killed in police raids or sent to prison on questionable charges of assault and murder. In the meantime, the mainstream civil rights movement, having succeeded in combating de jure (legalized) segregation, struggled to find ways to curtail economic discrimination and de facto (existing) segregation. Solutions seemed to become more elusive as large race riots erupted in cities across America from 1965 through 1968. On April 4, 1968 —a date that many historians implicitly accept as the end of the 1960s civil rights movement—Martin Luther King was assassinated. One week later, partly in tribute to the slain leader, Congress passed the Civil Rights Act of 1968, which outlawed discrimination in the sale and rental of most housing.

The Post–Civil Rights Era

After the end of the 1960s, civil rights supporters turned their attention to developing strategies that would counteract the lingering and often more subtle forms of racial bias in American institutions. The enforcement of antidiscrimination measures in employment and the establishment of affirmative action guidelines in workplaces and universities became the mainstay of civil rights advocacy in the last three decades of the twentieth century.

As early as 1953, the Presidential Committee on Government Contract Compliance had advised the Bureau of Employment Security to act "affirmatively to implement the policy of nondiscrimination." But the phrase "affirmative action" was not coined until 1961, when President Kennedy created the Equal Employment Opportunity Commission (EEOC) and urged contractors working on federally funded projects to "take affirmative action to ensure that applicants are employed without regard to race, creed, color, or national origin." Kennedy's directive was strengthened by the Civil Rights Act of 1964, which banned discrimination in the workplace and in public accommodations.

In 1965, President Lyndon Johnson ordered the enforcement of guidelines aimed at eliminating racial imbalance in hiring policies. By the early 1970s, these guidelines required employers to take positive steps to hire minorities by taking advantage of outreach and recruitment programs that helped to enlarge the minority applicant pool. In 1972, Congress passed the Equal Employment Opportunity Act, which allowed the EEOC to sue employers found guilty of discriminatory hiring practices. In 1975 the Supreme Court ruled that achieving a discrimination-free workplace could require companies to consider race as a factor when hiring new employees. And in 1980, the Supreme Court upheld the practice of setting aside 10 percent of public works contracts for businesses owned by minorities.

Through the mid-1970s, most of the legislation surrounding affirmative action emphasized the need to take aggressive steps to achieve racial diversity in workplaces and educational institutions. But from the late 1970s through the 1990s, lawmakers began to limit the scope of affirmative action as several individuals filed lawsuits claiming that such policies led to "reverse discrimination" against whites. In the 1978 case of *Regents of the University of California v. Bakke,* white college student Allan Bakke charged that the University of California at Davis denied him admission to its medical school because of his race. Bakke's lawyers maintained that the school's practice of retaining a certain number of slots for minority students discriminated against qualified white students. The Supreme Court eventually ruled that colleges may consider race in admissions decisions but may not set aside a fixed number of slots for minorities. Thus, the use of affirmative action quotas in hiring and college admissions was banned.

Several Supreme Court decisions in the 1990s continued to limit the scope of affirmative action. In 1995, for example, the Court struck down a decision in which a white contractor's low bid on a city construction project was rejected in favor of a Hispanic contractor's higher bid. The Hispanic contractor's bid had originally been accepted on affirmative action grounds as part of a policy requiring a certain percentage of public works projects to be awarded to minority-owned contracting firms. Although the Court had upheld such policies in 1980, its 1995 decision maintained that "equal protection of the law is a personal right, not a group right. Laws classifying citizens by race pose a great threat to that right."

In 1996, California voters approved a ballot measure that ended affirmative action programs in state hiring and public university admissions. The new law declared that the state could not "discriminate against or grant preferential treatment to any individual or group on the basis of race, sex, color, ethnicity, or national origin in the operation of public employment, education, and contracting." In 1997 the Supreme Court declined to review an appeals court ruling favoring the California initiative, a decision that allowed the anti–affirmative action measure to stand. The success of the California initiative has encouraged several other states to place anti–affirmative action measures on their ballots.

Many civil rights supporters are distressed by these rollbacks, arguing that affirmative action programs remain necessary because people of color still face discriminatory barriers in employment and education. According to a 1998 study conducted by the Fair Employment Council and Urban Institute, black and Hispanic job applicants encounter discrimination once in every five job applications. Lingering economic disparities are also cited as proof of a society that continues to operate to the advantage of whites and to the disadvantage of people of color: 30 percent of black households currently have incomes below the poverty line compared with 8 percent of white households, and the average black household income is only half that of the average white household income. Others, however, argue that the best way to change such statistics is not to enforce racial preferences but rather to remedy the social problems in minority families and communities. According to Roger Clegg, general counsel of the Center for Equal Opportunity, many people of color are not prepared to compete for good jobs "because of deteriorating family structure and [poor] public schools. Better to address these problems directly, rather than sweep them under the rug." When more minorities have stable family lives and high-quality education from an early age, Clegg contends, more of them will find lucrative work, with no need for racial preferences.

The Civil Rights Legacy

For many, the civil rights dream of full political and social equality between whites and blacks remains unfulfilled. Because patterns of de facto segregation in neighborhoods, schools, and social centers remain largely intact, many Americans people go through life with no significant or long-term contact with those of other races and are thus not afforded the perspective that could be gained from cross-racial interaction. Such a perspective, according to several of today's civil rights advocates, would lead to valuable understanding of continuing differences of opinion about the nature of racism, discrimination, and affirmative action in America.

Despite these persisting problems, the civil rights movement has profoundly transformed the American racial landscape. As a result of legal reforms fostered by the movement, more blacks and other minorities have access to high-quality education than ever before. This education is enabling them to enter an array of professional careers; many are also using their hard-won skills to help reduce racial inequities and develop strategies that promote social justice.

Since the late 1980s, moreover, hundreds of multiracial coalitions and organizations have emerged to fight institutional discrimination and encourage respectful communication between whites and people of color. The organization Building Just Communities, for example, was established in 1996 in Minneapolis to reverse that city's increasing level of poverty and racial segregation. In Cleveland, Ohio, a group of white and minority realtors formed the Residential Housing and Mortgage Credit Project, an effort to reduce barriers to racially equitable home ownership. In Flint, Michigan, the Community Enhancement Program has begun providing public forums to engage its citizens in dialogues on race.

Many of today's civil rights advocates maintain that the most pragmatic strategy is to remain optimistic about race relations and the potential for positive change. In a 1995 interview, author and former SCLC coordinator Maya Angelou emphasized the need to recognize the progress that has occurred since the Civil Rights Act of 1964:

> We've made a lot of progress—it's dangerous not to say so. Because if we say so, we tell young people, implicitly or explicitly, that there can be no change. Then they compute: "You mean the life and death and work of Malcolm X and Martin King, the Kennedys, Medgar Evers, Fannie Lou Hamer, the life and struggle of Rosa Parks—they did all that and *nothing has changed?* Well, then, what the hell am I doing? There's no point for me to do anything." The truth is, a lot has changed—for the good. And it's gonna keep getting better, according to how we put our courage forward, and thrust our hearts forth.

Chapter 1

The Struggle for Justice

EXAMINING ISSUES THROUGH
POLITICAL CARTOONS

Preface

The rights listed in the Declaration of Independence and the Constitution convey some of America's highest ideals, including liberty, autonomy, suffrage, freedom of expression, and equal protection under the law. For much of the nation's history, however, women and racial minorities were denied many of the constitutional rights that white men enjoyed: Women were not allowed to vote until 1920, and a deeply entrenched system of racial segregation excluded most minorities from mainstream society until the 1960s. Up through the middle of the twentieth century, for example, African Americans were denied access to certain public facilities —including hospitals, universities, and parks—and were granted admittance to "colored only" sections of buses, trains, dining rooms, bathrooms, and theaters. Most black children attended poorly funded segregated schools, and most black southerners were not allowed to vote. Those who openly opposed this unequal treatment usually faced brutal intimidation and violence.

In the 1960s, several grassroots organizations emerged to challenge legally enforced segregation and promote equal rights for African Americans. Inspired by the 1954 Supreme Court decision declaring segregated education unconstitutional and the successful 1955 boycott of segregated city buses in Montgomery, Alabama, groups such as the Congress of Racial Equality (CORE), the Southern Christian Leadership Conference (SCLC), and the Student Nonviolent Coordinating Committee (SNCC) organized sit-ins, demonstrations, marches, and voter-registration drives to counteract racial discrimination. Despite initial public resistance, the efforts of these groups transformed American society by dismantling officially sanctioned segregation and by removing barriers to black voting.

The civil rights movement of the 1960s compelled Americans to confront troubling realities about their imperfect democracy. The images in the following chapter document some of the substantial challenges and unsettling questions articulated during this struggle for justice.

Examining Cartoon 1:
"Let Freedom Ring!"

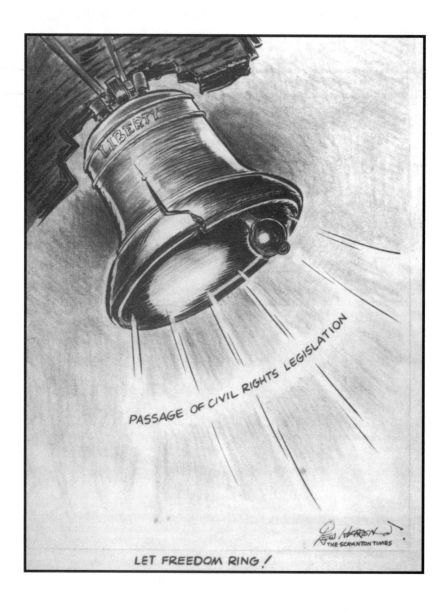

About the Cartoon

In this cartoon, the Liberty Bell, a historical symbol of American freedom and democracy, is depicted as reverberating with the "sound" of civil rights. The artist is celebrating the passage of the 1964 Civil Rights Act, which prohibited discrimination in public facilities and employment because of race, color, religion, sex, or national origin. The caption, "Let freedom ring!" explicitly connects the new legislation to Martin Luther King's famous "I Have a Dream" speech delivered after the August 28, 1963, March on Washington. That march, which drew over 250,000 people, had been organized as a show of support for the pending civil rights legislation. At the end of his speech, King uses the phrase—originally a line in the song "My Country 'Tis of Thee"—repetitively, imploring America to "let freedom ring from the prodigious hilltops of New Hampshire.... Let freedom ring from every hill and every molehill of Mississippi. From every mountainside, let freedom ring. When we let freedom ring ... we will be able to speed up that day when all of God's children, black men and white men, Jews and Gentiles, Protestants and Catholics, will be able to join hands and sing in the words of the old Negro spiritual, 'Free at last! Free at last! thank God Almighty, we are free at last!'"

About the Cartoonist

Lew Harsh drew editorial cartoons for the *Scranton Times* during the 1960s and 1970s.

Harsh. © Lew Harsh. Reprinted with permission.

Examining Cartoon 2:

"Pardon Me, Sir Why Are You Following Me?"

About the Cartoon

In the early 1960s, numerous sit-ins took place at segregated lunch counters and restaurants all over the South. Incorporating nonviolent tactics to protest racial segregation, black students, sometimes accompanied by whites, would politely order food and silently remain in their seats when they were refused service. In this cartoon, a white man walking to work is shadowed by a black character who mimics the white man's every move. Except for their race, the two characters appear identical. The black character declares that he is the white man's "social sit in," an integrator of people rather than places. The white man, apparently anxious about being seen at his workplace with an African American, tries to convince the black man that he is sympathetic to civil rights issues. But he reveals his true feelings when he rejects the black character's suggestion that he take "a colored person home" with him. The cartoonist is criticizing the hypocrisy of seemingly liberal whites who publicly claim to support civil rights and racial integration while remaining racially biased in their private day-to-day lives.

About the Cartoonist

Jules Feiffer, a native of New York City, created the weekly satirical comic strip *Sick, Sick, Sick,* (later entitled *Feiffer*), which appeared in the *Village Voice* for forty years and in the *London Observer* for over twenty years. *Feiffer* was nationally syndicated in 1959; other publications running the cartoonist's work include the *New Republic*, *Playboy*, *Esquire*, the *New Yorker*, the *Nation*, and the *New York Times*. Feiffer has also written several revues and plays, including the screenplays for the films *Carnal Knowledge* and *Popeye*. His many honors include the 1961 Academy Award for animation and the 1964 Pulitzer Prize for editorial cartoons.

Feiffer. © 1963, *The Village Voice*. Reprinted with permission.

Examining Cartoon 3:
"An' the Next Time . . ."

"An' the next time the gov'mint asks us if we have registered any niggras to vote we can look 'em right in the eye an' answer 'Yes'!"

About the Cartoon

The Fifteenth Amendment, adopted in 1879, made it illegal to deny any citizen the right to vote because of his or her race or former status as a slave. Between the 1890s and the 1960s, however, most African Americans in the South were barred from voting by the use of so-called poll taxes that individuals were required to pay before casting a vote. Southern registrars would also issue literacy tests to voters—with the intention of ensuring that blacks would not pass and not be allowed to vote. In the early 1960s, civil rights activists working to register black voters were met with rejection and violence in the South. However, after the passage of the 1965 Voting Rights Act, which prohibited poll taxes and literacy tests, black voter registration skyrocketed. This cartoon suggests that implacable racist officials in the South might still use trickery—by filling in registration forms with the names of deceased blacks—to circumvent the Voting Rights Act.

About the Cartoonist

Ollie Harrington was one of America's pioneering black cartoonists. Born in Valhalla, New York, he attended the Yale School of Fine Arts and the National Academy of Design, after which he worked for several major African American newspapers, including the *Pittsburgh Courier,* the *Amsterdam News,* and the *Chicago Defender.* His cartoon series *Dark Laughter* was the first black comic strip to receive national recognition. In the 1950s, Harrington moved to Europe, living as part of a group of African American expatriates that included the writers Chester Himes and Richard Wright.

Harrington. © *Daily World.* Reprinted with permission.

Examining Cartoon 4:
"The Victims"

THE VICTIMS

About the Cartoon

In the summer of 1965, a riot broke out in the Watts section of Los Angeles over accusations of police brutality against a black motorist. Riots and civil disturbances erupted during the next four summers in cities across the United States. The massive Newark and Detroit riots of the summer of 1967, during which this cartoon appeared, were the costliest up to that point in American history. These insurrections were, in part, the result of a growing anger that blacks felt over the federal government's failure to protect civil rights activists from brutal violence. Many African Americans, disillusioned with the tactics of passive resistance adopted by the movement led by Martin Luther King Jr., began to sympathize with the more militant and nationalist groups that promoted assertiveness and self-defense, such as the Nation of Islam and the Black Panthers.

The bird in the left lower corner of this cartoon, who questions the strategy espoused by black militants, represents the opinion of the cartoonist. In his opinion, the militant call to "get whitey"— that is, to take up arms against what some blacks see as an oppressive, white-controlled establishment—is connected with the rage that sparked the rioting. In addition, by depicting a black man looting a store labeled "civil rights"and presumably owned by an African American family, the cartoonist suggests that the lawlessness of the rioters only hurts other African Americans and undermines the struggle for civil rights.

About the Cartoonist

Pat Oliphant, a native of Adelaide, Australia, began his career at his hometown newspaper before moving to the United States in 1964. He started work as a political cartoonist at the *Denver Post* during that same year and became internationally syndicated in 1965. His awards include the Pulitzer Prize, two Reuben Awards, and the Best Editorial Cartoonist award from the National Cartoonists Society.

Oliphant © 1967, Universal Press Syndicate. All rights reserved. Reprinted with permission.

Examining Cartoon 5:
"Nobel Peace Prize"

About the Cartoon

Martin Luther King Jr. was awarded the Nobel Peace Prize in 1964; less than four years later, on April 4, 1968, he was assassinated in Memphis, Tennessee. This image of the award plaque pockmarked and cracked by a bullet symbolizes the sad paradox that was played out in the violent murder of a civil rights leader who advocated peace and nonviolence.

About the Cartoonist

Joaquin de Alba, born in Cadiz, Spain, studied drawing and painting at the School of Fine Arts in Seville. From 1936 to 1950, he worked as an editorial cartoonist for Francisco Franco's National Movement, the fascist political party that ruled Spain at that time. In 1951, disillusioned with Franco's repressive government, de Alba left Spain and worked in Latin America before moving to the United States in 1961. He became an editorial cartoonist for the *Washington Daily News*, often using his work to advocate democracy, freedom of conscience, and freedom of expression.

Joaquin de Alba. © 1969, Acropolis Books. Reprinted with permission.

Examining Cartoon 6:
"Blacks Only"

About the Cartoon

During the first half of the twentieth century, the words "colored" or "Negro" were commonly used to refer to Americans of African descent. By the later 1960s, many African Americans came to prefer the terms "Afro-American" or "black" as expressions of cultural pride, while "colored" and "Negro" were seen as the old-fashioned—and even somewhat discourteous—terms that whites used to describe blacks. This cartoon points to the irony inherent in society's use of the terms that blacks prefer even though blacks are still treated as second-class citizens. The white sign-painter is clearly irritated about having to keep changing the words, although he does nothing to challenge the segregation and unequal treatment represented by the separate drinking fountains. The suggestion is that society is unwilling to confront the deeper realities of racial discrimination. The segregated drinking fountain no longer existed when this cartoon was drawn—here the artist is likely using it as a symbol of the racism that he believes still pervades society at large.

About the Cartoonist

African American novelist and essayist Charles Richard Johnson signed up for a mail-order course in cartooning when he was thirteen years old. After creating comic strips for his high school and college newspapers, he became a regular editorial cartoonist for the Carbondale *Southern Illinoisian* and worked as a reporter and cartoonist for the *Chicago Tribune*. Johnson published his first novel in 1974; in 1990, he won the National Book Award for his critically acclaimed novel *Middle Passage*.

Johnson. © 1970, Johnson Publishing Company. Reprinted with permission.

Chapter 2

Has the Civil Rights Movement Benefited Minorities?

EXAMINING ISSUES THROUGH
POLITICAL CARTOONS

Preface

A nalysts can find many reasons to feel positive about the results of the civil rights movement. Statistics reveal that blacks and other minorities have made great strides since the passage of antidiscrimination laws nearly forty years ago. Today, for example, more than 30 percent of African Americans live in households that earn $35,000 per year or more, placing them solidly in the middle class. In the 1960s, less than 10 percent of blacks could be defined as middle class. The percentage of black college students jumped from 5 percent in 1960 to more than 11 percent in 1990. Furthermore, the number of black lawyers, engineers, doctors, entrepreneurs, and elected officials has dramatically increased since World War II: In 1940, less than 6 percent of African Americans held white-collar jobs, in comparison with about 50 percent today.

Despite these statistics, many experts maintain that minorities still encounter discrimination on a regular basis. According to a 1998 study conducted by the Fair Employment Council and Urban Institute, black and Hispanic job applicants encounter discrimination once every five times they apply for a job. A *Washington Post* poll conducted in 2001 reported that 35 percent of all blacks maintain that they have faced racial discrimination in the workplace—in comparison with 10 percent of all whites. Moreover, 66 percent of blacks do not believe that they have as good a chance as whites to get the type of job for which they are qualified. As one psychologist points out, "While whites are generally privileged or given the benefit of the doubt, too often persons of color are simply doubted." Sociology professor Bart Landry agrees: "[Discrimination] is still an obstacle. It just takes a more subtle form."

While the civil rights movement definitely opened up opportunities for minorities, some observers maintain that hidden forms of discrimination continue to make it difficult for minorities to achieve the kind of success that whites often take for granted. As the cartoonists in the following chapter suggest, the civil rights struggle is ongoing.

Examining Cartoon 1:
"A new study . . ."

About the Cartoon

Several studies conducted in the 1990s concluded that the quality of life for African Americans has greatly improved since the civil rights movement. Researchers Abigail and Stephan Thernstrom, for example, reported that while 87 percent of blacks lived in poverty in 1940, 75 percent of black married couples in the 1990s considered themselves middle class. Other statistics attest to increasing economic success among African Americans: Between 1970 and 1990, the number of black electricians grew from 14,145 to 43,276; bank tellers, from 10,633 to 46,332; and pharmacists, from 2,501 to 7,011. Such dramatic changes, analysts often contend, are largely the result of civil rights measures that have afforded blacks better opportunities for education and employment.

While these improvements have led many whites to conclude that discrimination is no longer an impediment to minority success, a majority of blacks believe that people of color still face myriad forms of discrimination and institutionalized racism. Often referred to as the racial "perception gap," this difference of opinion between whites and nonwhites is especially noticeable when examining public opinion on societal attempts to redress racism and discrimination. A 1997 Gallup poll revealed that more than 60 percent of whites believe that there are plentiful opportunities for blacks and that incidents of racial prejudice are rare. Sixty-seven percent of blacks, however, maintain that the government must continue to endorse policies that counteract discrimination.

Those who agree that racism still holds minorities back point to statistics that reveal continuing disparities between whites and blacks. For instance, about 30 percent of black households have incomes below the poverty line, in comparison to 8 percent of white households. Moreover, the average black household income is only half that of the average white household income. Many analysts maintain that while the quality of life for blacks has improved, racism can still thwart their chances for achievement, making it more difficult for them to attain the kind of success that whites often take for granted.

This cartoon, with its depiction of a white couple who are unable to see the various social problems that can hold minorities back, illustrates the idea of the racial "perception gap."

About the Cartoonist

Rob Rogers studied art at Oklahoma State University and received a master in fine arts at Carnegie-Mellon University in Pittsburgh, Pennsylvania, in 1984. He draws cartoons for the *Pittsburgh Post-Gazette*.

Rogers. © 1996, *Pittsburgh Post-Gazette*. Reprinted by permission.

Examining Cartoon 2:

"So How Come You People Are Still So Angry?"

About the Cartoon

After 1965, affirmative action policies were implemented to correct the effects of discrimination on women and people of color. The government took measures to increase minority representation in the U.S. workforce—typically by requiring companies to include race and gender as factors in hiring decisions. One negative side effect of affirmative action, as this cartoon suggests, is that businesses might employ and showcase "token" minorities as proof of their compliance with affirmative action policies. Thus, people of color may come to feel that they have been hired because of their minority status and not for their qualifications or talents. This cartoon sympathizes with "Joe Smith: Our Black Person," not only because has he been hired as a token, but also because he is confronted by a white coworker who apparently believes that minority anger over racial discrimination is no longer justified.

About the Cartoonist

Signe Wilkinson has drawn cartoons for several publications, including the *San Jose Mercury News* and *Organic Gardening Magazine*. She currently works full time as a cartoonist for the *Philadelphia Daily News*. Wilkinson is winner of the 1992 Pulitzer Prize for editorial cartooning and the 1997 Overseas Press Club Award.

Wilkinson. © 1997, Cartoonists & Writers Syndicate. Reprinted with permission.

Examining Cartoon 3:
"Equal Justice Under the Law"

About the Cartoon

This cartoon suggests that the criminal justice system in the United States fails to treat minorities fairly. A double standard in which whites receive equal justice while "coloreds" are prematurely condemned is likened to the pre–civil rights system of racial segregation that required whites and blacks to use separate facilities. The sketch appeared in the wake of several questionable shootings of minorities by police. In one high-profile case in 1999, African immigrant Amadou Diallo was shot nineteen times by four white New York City police officers. Diallo died instantly. The officers, who had been searching for a black suspect in a rape case, claimed they shot Diallo after confronting him because he reached into his pocket for his wallet—which they presumed was a gun. This incident occurred during a wave of public criticism of the criminal justice system. For example, several studies in the late 1990s concluded that minorities who have committed no crimes, especially African American males, are disproportionately stopped, searched, and detained by police. Many social analysts contend, moreover, that blacks are much more likely than whites to be brutalized or killed by police.

About the Cartoonist

Mike Thompson began his career at the *Milwaukee Journal* and later spent a brief stint at the *St. Louis Sun* before joining the Copley Illinois newspapers in 1990. Since 1998, he has drawn for the *Detroit Free Press.* His honors include the H.L. Mencken Award for cartooning, the Charles M. Schulz Award, and the Association of American Editorial Cartoonists' Locher Award.

Thompson. © 2000, Copley Media Services. Reprinted with permission.

Chapter 3

How Has Affirmative Action Affected Civil Rights?

EXAMINING ISSUES THROUGH
POLITICAL CARTOONS

Preface

Since the 1960s, the United States has used affirmative action to counteract the effects of discrimination on minorities and women—typically by adopting policies that increase female and minority representation in the workforce and in higher education. These policies were initiated as part of a larger plan to eradicate racial discrimination and poverty during President Lyndon Johnson's administration. In a 1965 speech, Johnson explained the rationale behind affirmative action: "You do not take a person who for years has been hobbled by chains and liberate him, bring him to the starting line and say you are free to compete with all the others." Civil rights leader Martin Luther King Jr. also emphasized this reasoning when he stated that "one cannot ask people who don't have boots to pull themselves up by their own bootstraps." A process that granted minorities some advantage in hiring decisions was seen as a vehicle for correcting centuries of injustice.

Contemporary defenders of affirmative action maintain that the policies have advanced the cause of civil rights by expanding employment and educational opportunities for minorities and women. They maintain, for example, that the increase in minority admissions at colleges has led to more lucrative career opportunities for people of color—which has in turn fostered a growing minority middle class. Many critics, however, contend that affirmative action hinders civil rights by encouraging employers and universities to select applicants on the basis of their minority status rather than their merit or ability. This leads to discrimination against whites, particularly white males, critics assert, as well as resentment and suspicion among those who feel that minorities are receiving unfair advantages. Such animosity can undermine the ideal of equal opportunity and hinder progress in race relations. According to Congressman Charles T. Canady, "The underlying purpose of preferences was to eliminate the vestiges of racism, [but] the mechanism was fundamentally flawed. Rather than breaking down racial barriers, preferential policies continually remind Americans of racial differences."

The cartoonists in the following chapter offer further commentary on the ethics and effectiveness of affirmative action.

Examining Cartoon 1:
"Roll It Back?!!....
How Come?...."

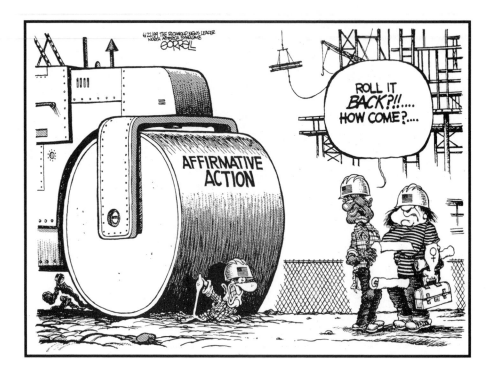

About the Cartoon

Affirmative action policies, which were first implemented after the passage of the Civil Rights Act of 1964, were intended to correct the effects of discrimination on women and minorities by requiring employers to take active measures to achieve gender and ethnic diversity in the workplace. By the late 1980s, when this cartoon appeared, critics of these measures were arguing that affirmative action had actually created a system of racial and gender preferences in employment. Opponents maintained that affirmative action led to the creation of a system of de facto "quotas" that forced employers to hire people based on their minority status, resulting in discrimination against qualified white males. Here the cartoonist argues that affirmative action must be scaled back by depicting it as a large steamroller about to completely flatten a struggling white male. The African American man and the feminist woman standing at a distance from the steamroller seem oblivious to the plight of the white male.

About the Cartoonist

The work of Bob Gorrell has appeared in more than four hundred newspapers and magazines, including *Time, Newsweek, U.S. News & World Report*, and *National Review*. He became an editorial cartoonist for the *Richmond (Virginia) News Leader* in 1983 and the *Richmond Times-Dispatch* in 1992. Since 1998, he has concentrated on drawing political cartoons for the Creators Syndicate. Gorrell has won several awards from the Virginia Press Association as well as the 1998 National Press Foundation Berryman Award for editorial cartoonist of the year.

Gorrell. © 1989, *Times Dispatch*. Reprinted with permission.

Examining Cartoon 2:
"How can you find any satisfaction . . ."

About the Cartoon

In this cartoon, a white man asks a minority woman if she can be content with her career success if she knows that she was hired because of her group affiliation and not because of her skills. Her response indicates that she believes that it is actually the white man who has received such "preferential treatment" over the course of his career. Affirmative action supporters often argue that white men have long had unfettered access to education and employment due to family ties, school connections, and personal referral networks that minorities usually lack. Preferential hiring of minorities, proponents contend, is the best way to correct the ongoing injustices that have resulted from decades of preferential hiring of whites.

About the Cartoonist

Clay Bennett worked as a staff artist for the *Pittsburgh Post-Gazette* before becoming a cartoonist for the *Fayetteville (North Carolina) Times* and the *St. Petersburg (Florida) Times.* Currently an editorial cartoonist for the *Christian Science Monitor,* his work is distributed throughout the United States.

Bennett. © Clay Bennett. Reprinted by permission of Christian Science Monitor.

Examining Cartoon 3:
"Gosh, It Works! . . ."

About the Cartoon

In 1996, California voters approved a ballot measure that ended affirmative action programs in state hiring and public university admissions. Its supporters were eager to adopt a new law declaring that the state could not "discriminate against or grant preferential treatment to any individual or group on the basis of race, sex, color, ethnicity, or national origin in the operation of public employment, education, and contracting." Affirmative action critics heralded the measure as a way to ensure fair and color-blind college admissions policies. However, in 1997, when the law went into effect, several California universities witnessed a sudden drop in minority enrollment—especially African American enrollment. This cartoon appeared at a moment when some experts were expressing concerns that the lack of minority representation on these campuses could create a stagnant learning environment that did not reflect the diversity of the outside world. The artist is here suggesting that "never noticing anyone's skin color" on campus would result from the exclusion of minorities rather than from a decrease in racism brought about by allegedly "color-blind" policies.

About the Cartoonist

A native of St. Louis, Missouri, Mike Peters joined the art staff of the *Chicago Daily News* in 1965. In 1966, he began a two-year stint of service with the U.S. Army as an artist for the Seventh Psychological Operations Group in Okinawa, Japan. He became an editorial cartoonist for the *Daily Dayton News* in 1969 and became nationally syndicated in 1972. Peters has authored several books of political cartoons and won several awards, including the 1981 Pulitzer Prize, the 1992 Reuben Award for cartoonist of the year, and the 1993 National Headliner Award.

Peters. © 1997, Tribune Media Services, Inc. All Rights Reserved. Reprinted with permission.

Chapter 4

What Is the Legacy of the Civil Rights Movement?

EXAMINING ISSUES THROUGH POLITICAL CARTOONS

Preface

Because it dealt a death blow to legalized racial segregation and black disfranchisement, most analysts see the 1960s civil rights movement as a proud chapter in American history. The movement not only changed laws and expanded opportunities for African Americans, it also inspired other late–twentieth century struggles for social justice, such as the feminist movement, the migrant farm laborer movement, and the gay and lesbian rights movement. Those who want to fight various forms of oppression and secure democratic freedoms for all people often look to the style and strategy of the civil rights movement for guidance and encouragement. Perhaps the movement's most enduring legacy, according to columnist E.J. Dionne Jr., is the conviction "that ordinary people [can] make a difference in the public sphere."

Some observers, however, contend that there are drawbacks to the civil rights legacy. The number of people seeking redress for past discrimination has increased, these observers maintain, and a "victim mentality," in which activists work to procure special rights for allegedly oppressed groups, has emerged. Some argue, for example, that the recent effort to pass a federal law prohibiting employment discrimination on the basis of sexual orientation is an attempt to grant homosexuals sympathy and political status as minorities in need of civil rights protections. Many conservatives insist that this measure is unnecessary—in their opinion, homosexuals have not been systematically denied employment in the same way that racial minorities and women have. While advocates for gays and lesbians see the struggle for the passage of a new antidiscrimination law as a genuine civil rights battle, critics assert that such a law would require employers to knowingly hire homosexuals, which they see as an infringement on the rights of businesses that support traditional moral values. As the conservative advocacy group Concerned Women for America argues, "an employer with moral or religious beliefs against homosexuality would be forced to lay down their *own* rights at the alter of the federal government."

In the following chapter, artists representing different points on the political spectrum present an array of opinions on the legacy of the civil rights movement.

Examining Cartoon 1:
"I Have a Dream. . . ."

About the Cartoon

In 1989, several civil rights organizations protested a series of six Supreme Court rulings that they believed would be harmful to the progress of blacks and other minorities in the workplace. In one of these cases, *Ward's Cove Packing Company v. Atonio*, the Court ruled that employers did not have to provide an explanation for hiring standards that appeared to be discriminatory. This decision reversed the 1971 *Griggs v. Duke Power Company* ruling, which required companies to prove that they were not discriminating if a plaintiff claimed that hiring practices did not reflect racial balance. Critics maintained that the *Ward's Cove* decision, along with five similar Court rulings in the late 1980s, would make it more difficult for minorities and women to demonstrate that an employer was engaging in discriminatory hiring policies.

On October 16 and 17 of 1990, the Senate and the House of Representatives each approved a bill intended to reverse those Court decisions. On October 22, however, President George Bush vetoed this bill, maintaining that it could lead to the return of hiring quotas in the workplace. Quotas—the establishment of a fixed number of minority positions in employment and college admissions—had been declared illegal in the late 1970s. Although companies could still consider race as a factor in hiring, they could no longer set aside a predetermined number of jobs for minorities.

After the veto of the 1990 legislation, the Bush administration participated in months of talks with both houses of Congress on several alternative civil rights bills. Eventually, the Civil Rights Act of 1991 was signed into law. This measure amended the 1964 Civil Rights Act to provide for damages in cases of intentional discrimination and unlawful harassment in the workplace.

This cartoon lampoons the process of the 1990 and 1991 civil rights legislation. Martin Luther King's simple and dignified "dream" is contrasted with Congress's messy political "nightmare" of a revised, amended, and constantly changing civil rights bill. The anonymous congressman holding the bill has a price tag on his head, suggesting that his input in the legislation is "for sale"— perhaps being "bid on" by competing interest groups.

About the Cartoonist

Nationally syndicated cartoonist Jeff MacNelly worked on the staffs of the *Richmond News Leader* and the *Chicago Tribune*. The winner of three Pulitzer Prizes for editorial cartooning, MacNelly is perhaps best known for his comic strip *Shoe*.

MacNelly. © 1991, *Chicago Times*. Reprinted with permission.

Examining Cartoon 2:
"Hold It!"

About the Cartoon

This cartoon is critical of the possibility that a seemingly endless number of special interest groups could eventually receive civil rights protection. Homosexuals are specifically focused on as a group that is about to board the "civil rights life raft" already occupied by ethnic and religious minorities and the disabled. Since the mid-1990s, advocates for gays and lesbians have lobbied for the Employment Non-Discrimination Act (ENDA), which would prohibit employment discrimination on the basis of sexual orientation. Supporters contend that such legislation would be an essential first step in securing equal rights for gays and lesbians. Critics, however, maintain that ENDA is unnecessary. Since homosexuality is not a visible trait, they argue, homosexuals do not meet the criteria for "minority status." The artist here laments the possibility that gays could be at the head of a long line of undeserving and allegedly "oppressed" groups that will end up competing for special treatment under the law.

About the Cartoonist:

Chuck Asay, a native of Alamosa, Colorado, decided he wanted to be a cartoonist when he was in the eighth grade. A two-time winner of the H.L. Mencken Award, Asay has worked as an editorial cartoonist for the *Colorado Springs Sun* and the *Colorado Springs Gazette Telegraph*. His work is nationally syndicated.

Asay. © *Colorado Springs Gazette Telegraph*. Reprinted with permission.

Examining Cartoon 3:

"The Thing That Strikes a Visitor to the South . . ."

About the Cartoon

In the late 1990s, a controversy erupted over the practice of flying the Confederate flag at government buildings and other public institutions in the South. Many African Americans are offended by this flag because it is a symbol of the pre–Civil War South with its system of slavery and subjugation of blacks. They contend that flying the flag at public buildings is a blatant form of racial insensitivity. Supporters of the Confederate emblem—some civil libertarians, others enthusiasts of southern culture—often maintain that the flag should simply be seen as a historical artifact. In the year 2000, the National Association for the Advancement of Colored People (NAACP) began a boycott of the state of South Carolina for its refusal to remove the flag from its capitol building. Other groups, such as the Southern Christian Leadership Conference, the National Governor's Association, and the Evangelical Lutheran Church of America, joined the boycott.

In this cartoon, the artist implies that promoters of the Confederate flag are attempting to deny its racist symbolism by arguing that the flag is an emblem of southern tradition and culture. The cartoonist obviously sympathizes with the NAACP and other participants in the South Carolina boycott—he shows actual bumper stickers that connect the image of the flag with sarcastic racial insensitivity, compares the "stars and bars" with the Nazi swastika, and suggests that the flag represents a shameful and violently racist history. The final panel is a reference to the presidential debates in the year 2000. During one debate, Republican candidate George W. Bush was asked what he thought about South Carolina's flying of the flag. Bush offered no personal opinion about the Confederate emblem, stating only that the people of South Carolina should determine the outcome of the controversy.

About the Cartoonist

Tom Tomorrow, a pseudonym for Dan Perkins, is the creator of *This Modern World*, a weekly cartoon of social and political satire that appears in approximately 120 newspapers across the country. His work has also been featured in journals such as the *Nation*, *U.S. News & World Report*, *Esquire*, and the *New Yorker*. Perkins is the recipient of numerous awards, including the 1998 Robert F. Kennedy Journalism Award for Cartooning, the Society of Professional Journalists' James Madison Freedom of Information Award, and, in the year 2000, the Professional Freedom and Responsibility Award given by the National Association for Education in Journalism and Mass Communication.

Tomorrow. © 1999, Tom Tomorrow. Reprinted with permission.

Examining Cartoon 4:
"Diverse Population Grows"

About the Cartoon

This cartoon is an imitation of Grant Wood's famous 1930 painting, *American Gothic*, which depicted a pitchfork-holding Iowa farmer and his aproned wife standing in front of a farmhouse with a gothic-style window. Here, an African American man and Asian woman stand in place of the white farmer and wife; the man carries a newspaper with a headline that reads, "Diverse Population Grows." The image is a reflection on demographic projections and census data that show an increase in the population of people of color in the United States. The cartoonist is perhaps also suggesting that today's minorities are experiencing increasing acceptance as full-fledged citizens—even to the extent of being perceived as "classic" or "typical"Americans. Diversity—one of the goals of the civil rights movement—is here revealed as a definitively American attribute.

About the Cartoonist

Steve Breen, a native of Huntington Beach, California, studied political science at the University of California in Riverside. He became a cartoonist for New Jersey's *Asbury Park Press* in 1996, and was nationally syndicated in 1997. In 2001, he joined the staff of the *San Deigo Union-Tribune* as a full-time editorial cartoonist. Breen won the 1998 Pulitzer Prize for editorial cartooning.

Breen. © 2001, Asbury Park Press. Reprinted by permission of Copley Media Services.

Chronology

April 12, 1861
Confederate troops fire on Union troops in Charleston, South Carolina, setting off the Civil War.

January 1, 1863
President Abraham Lincoln signs the Emancipation Proclamation, which frees all slaves held in the Confederate states.

April 1865
The Civil War ends with the defeat of the Confederacy; demanding equal rights, free blacks hold mass meetings throughout the South; on April 14 Lincoln is assassinated, and Andrew Johnson becomes president; southern legislatures begin to enact "black codes," which specify what sort of work African Americans may and may not do; these codes also establish penalties, including heavy labor, for black unemployment or vagrancy.

December 18, 1865
The Thirteenth Amendment, abolishing slavery everywhere in the United States, takes effect.

April 1866
A civil rights bill grants full citizenship to all citizens born in the United States (excepting Native Americans, who were not subject to taxes).

May 1866
Race riots occur in Memphis and New Orleans; homes, schools, and churches are burned; scores of blacks and their white supporters die.

March 2, 1867
Northern lawmakers pass the Reconstruction Act of 1867, which temporarily abolishes southern state governments, divides the South into Union-occupied districts, and gives African Americans the right to vote and hold political office.

1868
The Fourteenth Amendment makes all former slaves American citizens and requires that all citizens be granted equal protection of the law.

1869
The Fifteenth Amendment forbids states from denying male citizens the right to vote because of race, color, or former status as a slave; Ulysses S. Grant becomes president.

1870
The first black U.S. senator, Hiram R. Revels, is elected.

March 1, 1875
The Civil Rights Act of 1875 guarantees equal rights in public places without regard to color and forbids the exclusion of African Americans from jury duty; this law, however, does not apply to public schools.

March 27, 1876
In *United States v. Cruikshank*, the Supreme Court rules that the Fourteenth Amendment does not protect blacks from individual infringements on their rights, only from state infringements.

1877
Reconstruction ends on April 24; Rutherford B. Hayes becomes president.

1881
The "Jim Crow" era begins when Tennessee adopts a law requiring the separation of whites and blacks in railway coaches; other southern states soon follow suit, drafting legislation requiring racial segregation in schools, hospitals, transportation, and public accommodations; Chester A. Arthur becomes president after James A. Garfield is assassinated.

1883

The Supreme Court overturns the Civil Rights Act of 1875, holding that it is unconstitutional because it attempts to protect social rather than political rights.

1892

A record number of lynchings—241—occur.

1895

At his famous opening address at the Cotton States Exposition in Atlanta, black educator Booker T. Washington publicly rejects racial equality as an immediate solution to "the Negro problem"; he maintains that blacks must slowly earn civil rights through education and hard work.

1896

In *Plessy v. Ferguson*, the Supreme Court rules that state governments can segregate people of different races as long as "separate-but-equal" facilities are available. This ruling establishes a legal foundation for Jim Crow segregation until the middle of the twentieth century.

1898

In *Williams v. Mississippi*, the Supreme Court upholds the use of literacy tests and poll taxes as a prerequisite for voting; these requirements, applied in discriminatory ways, bar most southern blacks from voting.

1901

President William McKinley is assassinated; Theodore Roosevelt becomes president; the California legislature bans marriage between whites and Asians.

1905

W.E.B. Du Bois, the first African American to receive a Ph.D. from Harvard, establishes the Niagara Movement to protest increasing racial discrimination and to work to reestablish black voting rights; Booker T. Washington opposes this movement.

1909

Du Bois helps to found the National Association for the Advancement of Colored People (NAACP); the NAACP's purpose is to strengthen laws that protect the civil rights of African Americans; William Howard Taft becomes president.

1911
The National Urban League, an organization that focuses on the conditions of city-dwelling African Americans, is founded.

1913
Woodrow Wilson becomes president.

1915
Large numbers of African Americans begin migrating from the South to the North; in *Guinn v. United States*, the Supreme Court declares the "grandfather clause" unconstitutional; this clause had allowed states to use difficult registration tests to keep blacks from voting while exempting citizens—mostly white—whose grandfathers had voted.

1917
The United States enters World War I; the NAACP presses for racial equality through antidiscrimination lawsuits; in *Buchanan v. Warley*, the U.S. Supreme Court holds that state-mandated housing segregation is unconstitutional.

1918
World War I ends.

1919
Twenty-six race riots occur throughout the North and the South.

1920
The Nineteenth Amendment, granting women the right to vote, is ratified.

1923
Calvin Coolidge becomes president after Warren G. Harding dies in office.

1925
Asa Philip Randolph founds the Brotherhood of Sleeping Car Porters, the first national black labor union.

1928
Herbert Hoover is elected president; his running mate, Charles Curtis, becomes the first Native American vice president.

1929

The stock market crashes, setting off a worldwide economic depression; black activists in Chicago begin a Jobs for Negroes campaign, organizing a boycott against stores that do not hire African Americans.

1930

The NAACP mounts a successful campaign to defeat Hoover's nomination of Judge John J. Parker to the Supreme Court; Parker had a record of opposing black voting rights.

1932

Franklin D. Roosevelt is elected president.

1938

In the case of *Missouri ex rel. Gaines v. Canada*, the Supreme Court rules that the University of Missouri's practice of denying law-school admission to African American state residents is unconstitutional; the Court declares that Missouri must either admit African Americans to its state law schools or establish separate facilities for black law students.

1939

First Lady Eleanor Roosevelt resigns from the Daughters of the American Revolution (DAR) to protest their refusal to allow black contralto Marian Anderson to sing at Constitution Hall in Washington, D.C.; Roosevelt invites Anderson to sing at the Lincoln Memorial, attracting an audience of seventy-five thousand.

1941

Randolph proposes a march on Washington to protest the Roosevelt administration's lack of concern for civil right; Randolph calls off the march when Roosevelt issues an executive order outlawing race discrimination in defense-industry employment; the United States enters World War II.

1942

Many Japanese Americans are forced from their homes and are sent to internment camps in response to fears that they may be disloyal to the United States; in June the Congress of Racial Equality (CORE), committed to nonviolent direct action, is founded in Chicago by black and white civil rights leaders.

1943

On June 3, in an incident that became known as the Zoot Suit War, two hundred sailors wander the streets of Los Angeles, beating and stripping Mexican Americans wearing baggy pants and long jackets; the police arrest the Mexican Americans after they are beaten.

1944

In *Smith v. Allwright*, the Supreme Court strikes down a whites-only primary in Texas, declaring that the Fifteenth Amendment outlaws racial discrimination in primary elections.

1945

Roosevelt dies in office, and Harry S. Truman becomes president; World War II ends.

1946

The Tule Lake relocation center in California—the last of the Japanese internment camps—closes; in response to a series of race riots, Truman establishes the President's Committee on Civil Rights to determine how law enforcement "may be strengthened and improved to safeguard the civil rights of the people."

1947

On April 9 CORE sends the first integrated bus of Freedom Riders to challenge segregation in interstate travel in the upper South; they are arrested in North Carolina for violating the state's segregation laws.

1948

Truman orders an end to segregation in the U.S. armed forces.

1950

The Korean War begins.

1952

Dwight D. Eisenhower is elected president.

1953

The Korean War ends.

1954

On May 17, in *Brown v. Board of Education*, the Supreme Court declares that racially segregated public education is unconstitutional.

1955

A fourteen-year-old black youth, Emmett Till, is lynched in Mississippi for saying "hey, baby" to a white woman; Till's mother has an open-casket funeral so that the public and the media can see the boy's badly mutilated body.

May 1955

The Supreme Court tempers its *Brown* ruling by demanding no timetable for school desegregation, only that districts comply "with all deliberate speed."

December 1, 1955

In Montgomery, Alabama, a former NAACP field secretary, Rosa Parks, is arrested for refusing to give up her bus seat to a white passenger; her arrest triggers a yearlong boycott of the city's bus system, led by recently ordained Baptist minister Martin Luther King Jr.

January 5, 1956

Eisenhower calls for "equal pay for equal work without discrimination because of sex" in his state-of-the-union speech.

March 12, 1956

Southern senators and representatives declare that they will use "all lawful means" to reverse the Supreme Court's 1954 decision to desegregate public schools.

September 10, 1956

Public schools in Louisville, Kentucky, are racially integrated; the National Guard is dispatched to protect black students attending newly integrated schools in Kentucky and Tennessee.

November 1956

Californian Dalip Singh Saund becomes the first Asian American elected to Congress.

February 14, 1957

The Southern Christian Leadership Conference (SCLC) is founded under the leadership of Martin Luther King Jr.; the SCLC advocates a combined strategy of nonviolent direct action, litigation, boycotts, and voter registration to end segregation.

September 1957

Congress passes the Civil Rights Act of 1957, which gives the U.S. attorney general greater power to enforce the desegregation of public schools; the act also establishes a new Civil Rights Commission and requires federal rather than state enforcement of voting rights.

September 24, 1957
Arkansas governor Orval Faubus calls out the National Guard to prevent the integration of Little Rock's Central High School; in response, Eisenhower orders federal troops to enforce the school district's desegregation order.

June 26, 1959
Virginia's Prince Edward County closes its public school system to prevent the racial integration of its schools.

February 1, 1960
The sit-in movement begins in Greensboro, North Carolina, when four black college students quietly refuse to leave a Woolworth's lunch counter after being denied service; in the following week, CORE helps demonstrators organize sit-ins in fifteen southern cities.

Spring 1960
The Student Nonviolent Coordinating Committee (SNCC) is founded in Raleigh, North Carolina, by activists involved in the lunch-counter sit-ins; a grassroots organization, SNCC's original intention is to nonviolently confront all forms of racial segregation.

May 6, 1960
The Civil Rights Act of 1960, which authorizes federal judges to appoint mediators to help African Americans register to vote, is signed into law.

November 1960
John F. Kennedy is elected president.

1961
Kennedy creates the Equal Employment Opportunity Commission (EEOC) and urges federally funded contractors to "take affirmative action to ensure that applicants are employed without regard to race, creed, color, or national origin."

May 1961
CORE director James Farmer and a racially mixed group of Freedom Riders organize a bus trip through the Deep South to test the

region's compliance with desegregation ruling; one bus is firebombed in Anniston, Alabama; all passengers escape without serious injury; SNCC then takes over the organization of the Freedom Rides.

September 30, 1962
Federal marshals escort black air force veteran James Meredith as he registers for admission to the University of Mississippi; a riot ensues, during which two people die.

April/May 1963
King and other civil rights leaders begin a campaign to desegregate public facilities in Birmingham, Alabama; police chief Eugene "Bull" Connor turns fire hoses and police dogs on nonviolent demonstrators; and many activists are beaten and arrested; the violence, which is broadcast on the national news, shocks Americans.

June 11, 1963
Kennedy asserts federal control over the Alabama National Guard after the state's governor, George C. Wallace, refuses to allow the integration of the University of Alabama.

June 12, 1963
Medgar Evers, field director of the Mississippi NAACP, is assassinated.

August 28, 1963
More than 250,000 demonstrators participate in the March on Washington in support of civil rights; the march culminates in King's "I Have a Dream" speech.

September 1963
Four black girls are killed in the bombing of the Sixteenth Street Baptist Church in Birmingham, Alabama; Ku Klux Klan members are among the suspects in the bombing.

November 22, 1963
Kennedy is assassinated; Lyndon B. Johnson becomes president.

1964
Congress passes the Civil Rights Act of 1964, which forbids discrimination in jobs, housing, and public accommodations because of race, color, religion, sex, or national origin.

Summer 1964

SNCC invites more than one thousand northern students to help register black voters in Mississippi and to teach in their "freedom schools"; on August 4 the bodies of three SNCC workers—Michael Schwerner, James Chaney, and Andrew Goodman—are discovered near Philadelphia, Mississippi; the Ku Klux Klan and local police are implicated in their deaths.

October 15, 1964

King receives the Nobel Peace Prize.

1965

Congress passes the Voting Rights Act, which strengthens federal authority to ensure the right to vote and to counter discriminatory practices by local election officials; President Johnson orders the enforcement of guidelines aimed to eliminate racial imbalance in hiring—the first affirmative action policy; in February black nationalist leader Malcolm X is assassinated; from August 11 to 16, a major race riot occurs in the Watts section of Los Angeles; other riots ensue in other cities over the next three years.

1966

Feminist leader Betty Friedan founds the National Organization for Women (NOW); the organization, inspired by the black civil rights movement, aims to push for "full equality for women in America in a truly equal partnership with men."

June 1966

On a march through Mississippi with King, SNCC activist Stokely Carmichael calls for "black power"—an idea that embraces "whatever means necessary," even violence, to combat racial discrimination; after a discussion with King, Carmichael agrees not to use the slogan during the rest of the march.

July 1, 1966

CORE endorses the concept of black power; the NAACP and SCLC reject this concept.

December 1966

SNCC adopts the concept that black separatism, not integration, is required to garner rights for African Americans; it expels whites from its organization.

April 15, 1967
King delivers a speech linking the civil rights movement with the movement against the war in Vietnam.

June 12, 1967
In *Loving v. Virginia*, the Supreme Court rules that laws banning interracial marriage are unconstitutional.

June 13, 1967
NAACP attorney Thurgood Marshall becomes the first African American to serve on the Supreme Court.

August 1967
FBI director J. Edgar Hoover launches a counterintelligence program to "expose, disrupt, misdirect, discredit, or otherwise neutralize" radical black liberation groups.

October 1967
In Oakland, California, Huey Newton and Bobby Seale found the Black Panther Party, a militant black nationalist organization; the group's original intention is to emphasize black self-defense.

February 1968
SNCC merges with the Black Panthers.

April 1968
King is assassinated on April 4; riots occur in 125 cities and thirty-eight people die; Congress passes the Civil Rights Act of 1968, which bans discrimination in the sale and rental of most housing.

July 1968
CORE becomes a black nationalist organization and expels its white members.

August 1968
SNCC disassociates itself from the Black Panthers and expels Stokely Carmichael.

November 1968
The Black Panthers welcome whites as partners in the black liberation struggle, but it maintains that blacks must lead the movement; Richard M. Nixon is elected president.

January 3, 1969

Shirley Chisholm becomes the first African American woman elected to Congress.

June 28, 1969

Gays and lesbians battle against a police raid on the Stonewall Inn, a gay bar in New York City; the riot marks the beginning of a movement in which gays and lesbians demand civil rights and greater societal acceptance of homosexuality.

1971

In *Sumner v. Charlotte-Mecklenburg Board of Education*, the Supreme Court rules that cross-district busing and racial quotas are permissible means of integrating schools.

1972

Congress passes the Equal Employment Opportunity Act, which allows citizens to sue companies with discriminatory hiring practices; Title IX of the Educational Amendments Act calls for equal opportunities for male and female students in schools that receive federal funding; in March, Congress also passes the Equal Rights Amendment (ERA), which declares that women and men are granted "equality of rights under the law"; the ERA is never ratified, however, because it fails to achieve passage in the required number of state legislatures.

1974

In *Milliken v. Bradley*, the Supreme Court declares that multidistrict school desegregation plans may involve only districts that have themselves discriminated; this ends busing between most urban and suburban districts; Nixon resigns from office, and Gerald Ford becomes president.

November 1976

Jimmy Carter is elected president.

June 28, 1978

In *Regents of the University of California v. Bakke*, the Supreme Court rules that although publicly funded schools may use race as a factor in admissions decisions, they cannot set aside a fixed number of slots for minorities.

April 11, 1980

The Equal Employment Opportunity Commission (EEOC) issues guidelines banning sexual harassment in the workplace.

November 1980

Ronald Reagan is elected president.

July 7, 1981

Sandra Day O'Connor becomes the first female Supreme Court Justice.

1988

Congress passes legislation officially apologizing for the internment of Japanese Americans during World War II, and twenty thousand dollars is given to each surviving relocation victim; George Herbert Walker Bush is elected president.

1989

In *Richmond v. J.A. Croson Company*, the Supreme Court overturns a Richmond, Virginia, affirmative action plan that set aside a certain percentage of city works projects for minority contractors.

1990

The Americans with Disabilities Act is signed into law; this act bans disability-based discrimination in employment, government services, and public facilities.

1991

The Civil Rights Act of 1991 is passed; this measure clarifies and expands the rights of job-discrimination victims to sue; Clarence Thomas, a black conservative Supreme Court nominee, is accused of having sexually harassed a former employee while he was head of the EEOC during the 1980s; following heated nationally televised hearings, the Senate confirms Thomas as a justice.

1992

In Los Angeles a jury acquits four white police officers of brutality charges in the videotaped beating of black motorist Rodney King; the verdict sparks four days of riots in which more than fifty people are killed; four white students sue the University of Texas law school for reverse discrimination, claiming that they had been denied admission so that less-qualified minorities could attend the school; eventually an appeals court rules that the school can no longer elevate some races over others in its admissions policies; Bill Clinton is elected president.

1994
Under the "don't ask, don't tell" policy, the U.S. armed forces are no longer to investigate or ask recruits about their sexual orientation; although homosexual behavior is still grounds for dismissal, homosexual orientation by itself is not.

1996
Californians approve a ballot measure that ends affirmative action programs in state hiring and public university admissions; Clinton signs the Defense of Marriage Act, which forbids federal recognition of same-sex marriages and gives states the right to refuse to recognize gay marriages performed in other states.

1998
The United States officially apologizes for conducting secret medical experiments on four hundred black men earlier in the century; between 1932 and 1972, these men had been denied treatment for syphilis to study how the disease progressed; financial reparations are paid to them and their heirs.

May 1999
In *Aurelia Davis v. Monroe County Board of Education*, the Supreme Court rules that school districts may be held liable for student-on-student sexual harassment.

For Further Research

Barry D. Adam, *The Rise of a Gay and Lesbian Movement*. New York: Twayne, 1995.

Maurianne Adams et al., eds., *Readings for Diversity and Social Justice: An Anthology on Racism, Sexism, Anti-Semitism, Heterosexism, Classism, and Ableism*. New York: Routledge, 2000.

Jules Archer, *They Had a Dream: The Civil Rights Struggle from Frederick Douglass to Marcus Garvey to Martin Luther King and Malcolm X*. New York: Puffin, 1996.

Annie S. Barnes, *Everyday Racism: A Book for All Americans*. Naperville, IL: Sourcebooks, 2000.

Bob Blauner, *Still the Big News: Racial Oppression in America*. Philadelphia: Temple University Press, 2001.

William G. Bowen and Derek Curtis Bok, *The Shape of the River: Long-Term Consequences of Considering Race in College and University Admissions*. Princeton, NJ: Princeton University Press, 1998.

Eric Brandt, ed., *Dangerous Liaisons: Blacks, Gays, and the Struggle for Equality*. New York: New Press, 1999.

Jim Carnes, *Us and Them: A History of Intolerance in America*. New York: Oxford University Press, 1999.

Clayborn Carson, *In Struggle: SNCC and the Black Awakening of the 1960s*. Cambridge, MA: Harvard University Press, 1981.

Ed Clayton, *Martin Luther King: The Peaceful Warrior*. Ed. Pat MacDonald. New York: Archway, 1996.

Samuel Cohn, *Race and Gender Discrimination at Work*. Boulder, CO: Westview Press, 2000.

Ward Connerly, *Creating Equal: My Fight Against Racial Preferences*. San Francisco: Encounter Books, 2000.

Sara Evans, *Personal Politics: The Roots of Women's Liberation in the Civil Rights Movement and the New Left*. New York: Knopf, 1979.

Linda George and Charles George, *Civil Rights Marches*. Danbury, CT: Childrens Press, 1999.

Scott Gillam, *Discrimination: Prejudice in Action*. Springfield, NJ: Enslow, 1995.

Peter Irons, *A People's History of the Supreme Court: The Men and Women Whose Cases and Decisions Have Shaped Our Constitution*. New York: Penguin, 1999.

Alvin M. Josephy Jr., ed., *Red Power: The American Indians Fight for Freedom*. Lincoln: University of Nebraska Press, 1985.

Martin Luther King Jr., *Why We Can't Wait*. New York: Harper & Row, 1963.

Elisabeth Lasch-Quinn, *Race Experts: How Racial Etiquette, Sensitivity Training, and New Age Therapy Hijacked the Civil Rights Revolution*. New York: W.W. Norton, 2001.

Peter B. Levy, *The Civil Rights Movement*. Westport, CT: Greenwood, 1998.

Christopher Martin, *Mohandas Gandhi*. Minneapolis: Lerner, 2000.

Carlos Munoz Jr., *Youth, Identity, Power: The Chicano Movement*. New York: Verso, 1989.

Diane Silver, *The New Civil War: The Lesbian and Gay Struggle for Civil Rights*. Danbury, CT: Franklin Watts, 1997.

Leonard Steinhorn and Barbara Diggs-Brown, *By the Color of Our Skin: The Illusion of Integration and the Reality of Race*. New York: Penguin, 1999.

Anthony Stith, *Breaking the Glass Ceiling: Sexism and Racism in Corporate America: The Myths, Realities, and the Solutions*. Toronto: Warwick, 1998.

Stephan Thernstrom and Abigail Thernstrom, *America in Black and White: One Nation, Indivisible.* New York: Simon and Schuster, 1997.

Becky W. Thompson, *A Promise and a Way of Life: White Antiracist Activism.* Minneapolis: University of Minnesota Press, 2001.

Juan Williams, *Eyes on the Prize: America's Civil Rights Years, 1954–1965.* New York: Penguin, 1987.

Index